OUTSTANDING

A Leader's Guide
to Effective
CQC Registration

TARUNA CHAUHAN

RƎTHINK PRESS

First published in Great Britain in 2019 by Rethink Press
(www.rethinkpress.com)

Cover image © Shutterstock.com | ArthurStock

Praise

'Taruna Chauhan's book provides
detailed information that will help
a provider through the application
process. I really enjoyed reading it – so
much so that I've read it twice!'
— Geri Connelly

Contents

*To my parents who both had an
entrepreneurial spirit, and my husband Jay
and children Jyoti and Viraj who have always
supported me in my business journey.*

Foreword

Seven years ago I decided to start my own healthcare company. It was a bold and optimistic vision, but it was soon tempered by the stark realities of creating a start-up. As a consultant physician, I was knowledgeable in my field of infectious diseases but I just didn't know 'how' to start a business. Worse still, I was informed that our Travel Health Clinic would need to be regulated by the Care Quality Commission.

Following a hasty call to the CQC, I was directed to a maze-like website. It was terrifying. Suddenly I felt rather lonely and helpless, like a ship in a vast ocean without a map, oars, sails or a compass. It turned out to be a cumbersome, arduous, time-consuming and energy-sapping journey. I wished I had had a guide, an experienced and knowledgeable teacher holding my hand and taking me through the uncharted waters safely.

Outstanding is that map and Taruna Chauhan is your guide. The book starts by helping you find out 'why' you are doing what you are. Then it will take you through the application process in a series of logical steps. *Outstanding* addresses the key principles the CQC uses to assess new organisations, ie SCREW – is the organisation Safe, Caring, Responsive, Effective and Well-led? Planning and preparation is vital for both the registration and subsequent inspections, and this is also covered in the final chapter of the book.

I have known Taruna for five years. Her skills have been honed for many years, including spending a number of years in a teaching hospital in the NHS as a quality manager. When Travel Klinix won a tender with Coventry City Council to start an innovative community screening project, we turned to Taruna for her clinical governance expertise to ensure standards and key quality benchmarks were achieved. She helped us train new volunteers and ensured appropriate policies were fit for purpose and the council's exacting quality standards were achieved. Our partnership culminated in the project achieving national recognition for innovation and quality of care of patients by the Royal College of Physicians.

Outstanding is your essential guide to navigating the CQC application process. It will take you from the inception of your business concept to the dreaded interview, where your organisation and your services will be closely scrutinised by the CQC inspector. *Outstanding* will help you lose the dread of CQC regulation and save you many sleepless nights.

Dr Ravi Gowda

Consultant in Infectious Diseases and Director of Travel Klinix, MBBS, MRCP(UK), MRCGP, DCH, DRCOG, DFFP, DTM&H

www.travelklinix.com

Introduction

Towards the end of their lives my parents both had care at home. The care they received was varied. In the early days there were mishaps in the carers' understanding of what we wanted for my parents, and us knowing what needed to be explained to the carers.

In my opinion, the company did not care about person-centred care. We had short visits which the organisation thought was adequate to warm up their lunch in the microwave and give them their medication. Weekends were the worst as the carers changed often. Also, rather than being encouraged to become independent after a fall, Mum was actually encouraged to use a commode to the extent that she lost all confidence and never walked to the bathroom again. It broke my heart, but I was two hours' drive away and only able to help my sister with respite care.

After many years in quality management for the NHS, I decided to start my consultancy business with a view to supporting the providers to do a better job through creating efficient processes and recruiting staff with strong values. These values include a passion to work in the sector, a capable approach, positive attitude and sense of compassion, so that the people who use services received person-centred care or treatment.

I have supported home care agencies, hair transplant clinics, aesthetics clinics and urgent care clinics. I am currently mentoring a homecare group after transformation, which is another of my services.

My support for new providers in their Care Quality Commission (CQC) application aims to encourage providers of a regulated activity to start on the right path with both business and mindset. A business is more likely to succeed if the right processes are in place and the values are embedded within the organisation. While I support them with the application to ensure they receive their validation to carry on a regulated activity, I also encourage them to look at the bigger picture, not just compliance with CQC.

The reason for writing this guide is twofold. Firstly, I want to support those completing an application themselves to do so efficiently and with all the information in place so that when they start the actual online application, they can do so in one sitting. The CQC website is not the easiest to navigate so I hope that this guide will make it easy for you to gather all the relevant information and increase your chances of success.

Secondly, the book aims to root out those who are not yet ready to start a regulated activity and will need to go through the process of personal development required and may decide that perhaps it is not for them. For example, a company I supported with their application decided later, when the CQC asked for further information, that they did not want the added burden. They could have saved themselves money if they had known the level of information and processes the CQC requires earlier in the process.

I want this guide to be the go-to resource for people starting a CQC-regulated activity. The

CQC application uses two handbooks for the two frameworks: Healthcare (which encompasses primary care, acute care, dentists, GPs etc) and Adult Social Care (which includes care homes, homecare agencies, supported living etc). You choose the one relevant to your business and use this as a basis for your application. There is additional information to look at on the CQC website in relation to such areas as primary care and specialist services. This means spending time on the website and gleaning what you need from it.

This book should enable any provider, whether in the health or care sector, to follow the steps to an outstanding application which is validated.

ONE

Having a CQC-Regulated Business

New providers need to think about why they are opening a care business. Is it to just make a profit or is it for some altruistic reason? My clients have had many reasons. One client started their business because they wanted to do something meaningful and felt a care business would provide this. Another client started theirs because they looked after people with learning disabilities and, as they were long-term clients, they increasingly required personal care, which is a regulated activity. One of my clients has a private transport service. They started their own company because they wanted to run a firm which had more ethical values.

Running a regulated company is difficult. There are twenty regulations to meet, plus running the core business itself. It is difficult to understand what is required for achieving compliance and running a business if you are new to the sector. I have people such as nurses who come to me and do not know about the CQC standards to the depth I would expect them to. This is concerning in light of the information supplied and available.

Running a regulated activity

In the health sector, the emphasis is on needing to register because you are undertaking activities which are regulated by the CQC. The business is usually up and running for non-regulated activity and the regulated activity is an add-on. Or, in the instance of Polydioxanone (PDO) thread lifts, (a treatment which lifts and tightens sagging skin tissue, using threads made of PDO introduced into the deeper layers of the skin), the CQC possibly decided that this would *become* a regulated activity. As far as I know there was no consultation or announcement, it just trickled into the knowledge of the aesthetics clinics. I even had to phone the CQC to get this confirmed, before supporting a client with their CQC application. However, I am pragmatic, as are the clinics who carry out regulated activities.

What is your WHY?

Running a business is hard. No business runs smoothly, and it is at times like these you need to know what your WHY is so that you can carry on, even through the difficult times. There are many variables to consider. These days, even obtaining a council contract is not as easy as it was in the past. In some cases, the council will not identify a new provider as a supplier until they have had their first CQC inspection. I think this stems from when it was easy to start a business – they had many new providers who did not meet the standards. Therefore, it is important to understand what is required in running a regulated organisation.

You need to think about the model for your business. Will it be homecare, supported living/ domiciliary care or a residential care home?

Clinics

In carrying out regulated activities, and here I am writing about those clinics which perform regulated treatments such as hair transplants or PDO thread lifts, the clinic will carry out both regulated and non-regulated treatments.

Any regulated activity will have criteria to meet which can be used in the other treatments as it will be good practice in these areas as well.

New providers also need to know how to run a business. Many new providers I work with have been carers who now feel they can go it alone. They have the caring background but do not realise what is required in terms of running a robust business with processes while meeting compliance standards and the needs of individuals.

New providers, or those who now carry out a regulated activity, come to me for support to write their application. Some come to me from the beginning, others come because they have been rejected and need help to make a successful application. Or they get stuck part-way through the application process. New providers are not often aware of the CQC Key Lines of Enquiry (KLOE) and some have not even accessed the CQC website for guidance, or, where they have, vital information has been missed.

I had an organisation come to me which had been rejected for registering a supported living application. When I looked at the application it was poorly written with references to the care home business and nothing to do with supported living. I was even more surprised when I mentioned the KLOE and SCREW – they said they did not know what I was referring to.

KLOE stands for Key Lines of Enquiry; SCREW stands for Safe, Caring, Responsive, Effective and Well-led. This provider had been running its care business for many years and therefore I would have expected it to have continuous improvement as part of its development.

I have even given a refund to one client because, after starting their application, it soon became clear to me that they would be rejected once again because they did not have the depth of knowledge and skill to be a registered manager of care services. They had led me to believe that this was because the husband had completed the application and he didn't know the sector very well. The application would not have been successful even with my support, as they were not prepared to do any extra training that would have helped. I work with integrity and have the same expectation of my clients. Clients must be prepared to put the work in.

TWO

Steps Before Your Application

To get clarity on your business I am going to introduce you to the 'Strategy on a Page' (SOAP) methodology as it will give you a great way to look at your business.

SOAP is a method devised by Deri ap John Llewellyn Davies from his book *BGI Strategy On a Page*. The details are at the back of this book should you wish to purchase a copy. It is an easy reference book. I use it with my mentor clients as it enables them to look at their business 'on a page'.

I use the SOAP methodology because I like the simplicity of the method. I have created my own simple table for my clients which allows them to break down their strategy into Vision, Purpose, Values, Monthly Goals and Key Actions.

With this tool you can look at your business in a 12-month period and then break it down into 6-month and 3-month goals so that you can see where the business is going and how it aligns with the CQC standards. You need to remember the standards are a part of the business and not the only thing, as you need to market your business, complete tenders to the local authority and make yourself the provider of

Table 2.1 Business Strategy On A Page

Vision	Purpose	Values	Monthly goals	Key Actions
Your unique selling point (USP), your place in the marketplace, company promise. What type of people will you need to deliver your vision? Your brand is a visual representation of your vision.	Your reason for being.	Principles that you run your organisation by. **Must be lived every day from owner to staff.**		
Long-term strategy: 12 months Marketing strategy Quality assurance Pillars: finance, planning, marketing sales and human resources.	**Medium-Term Strategy:** 6 months	**Short-term Strategy:** 3 3months		

choice. You also need to ensure you have appropriate insurance in place for the activity you do and think about HM Revenue and Customs (HMRC), pensions and accounting, also about the General Data Protection Regulation (GDPR).

Vision

Think about your vision for the business. What's the big vision you have? Where do you see your business in five years' time?

It is useful to ask yourself these questions:

- Why do you exist?

- What is your company/organisation aiming to do?

Purpose

In SOAP, 'purpose' is made up of five areas:

1. Passion

2. Service and value

3. Opportunity

4. Financial reward

5. Lifestyle

1 Passion

You need to love what you do because when you have plateaus in the business or bad days it is the passion for your business which will carry you through. Look at what you really enjoy doing. How does it make you feel? For instance, I love mentoring. I get so much satisfaction out of the light-bulb moment or the smile when I suggest a small tweak that can make a big difference: that's what gets me up in the morning.

2 Service and value

Are you going to be of service and add value? By serving others well and giving them value we get so much, it's not just about financial rewards. It's about how it makes you feel, how it makes your client feel. I will give you an example of a restaurant we went to in Bicester. I am intolerant to wheat so I needed to know that the dishes I wanted to choose were indeed wheat-free. I was really impressed by my server as she knew the ingredients and what the dishes came with. She didn't have to go and ask the chef. For dessert, my husband was going to choose Black Forest gateau. I happened to ask if it contained beef gelatine. The woman said if you don't eat beef gelatine the Black Forest gateau is not suitable because the cherry filling has gelatine in it. She clearly had good training.

3 Opportunity

In the health and care sector, there is a great opportunity and there is a buoyant market. However, you still need to research the market in your area.

How will you be able to get clients in your area? For example, in Coventry the county council will not give contracts to new providers of social care. They will only allow them on the suppliers list after the first inspection. New providers must look for opportunities with private clients, which means they need to really think about their marketing strategy. You can ask a private client for greater fees, but you do need to provide a premium service. You cannot provide a premium service on the council rates as the new provider has to provide a service which is fit for purpose and is not losing the organisation money. You need to think outside the box and provide a service which is value-added.

4 Financial reward

We go into business to enable us to pay the bills. However, it's no use setting up your business if you can't then have the lifestyle you want or are accustomed to. It's important to consider the cost of the lifestyle you want, how you can achieve it and how long it will take. In the beginning you will put in long hours, but you need to know what steps to take to enable you to have the financial reward you want and work the hours to suit your lifestyle.

5 Lifestyle

It's important to think about this as it will impact on what you do in your business.

What do you want from your life? I lead an integrated lifestyle where I consistently mix business and personal. I work from home and do a lot of work online with my clients, yet I work nationally also. I have business friends all over the world. I love going on long-haul holidays and meeting my friends when I want to: but it's so easy to start doing before thinking.

Think about your vision for the business. Think big: your vision coupled with your purpose will drive your strategy. Where do you want to be in two years, or five years, from now?

What does your exit strategy look like? You are probably wondering why I am asking about your exit plan when you are just embarking on your business journey. The reason is that if you don't know what your exit plan is, how will you know when you are there? And more importantly, how are you going to plan for it? Davies talks about this in his book and I think it is important to think about. Too many businesses fail to incorporate it into their thinking and when they get to the point where they want to retire, they can't because they have not completed an exit plan. Don't assume that if you have children, they will necessarily want to take over the family business. How will you find the right person to take over? You need to think about **succession planning**. I recently helped a care home to put in an application for a registered manager job-share because the owner was the registered manager and he wanted to reduce his hours and semi-retire. His office manager, who did a lot of the work and had the right skills, is now doing the job-share so that he can mentor her to take the reins. This is a good example of succession planning.

You need the right succession plan and that needs to be in place years before you want to exit the business.

To help you with your business SOAP, answer the following questions:

1. What does success look like?

2. Who is with you?

3. Where are you?

Think about your brand. What does it stand for? What are the values attached to this? A good organisation to look at in this sector is Home Instead, (www.homeinstead.co.uk) a homecare agency franchise which has a clear brand value, vision and mission. You need to think about how you want your organisation to be perceived in the future. Look at your competitors and look at their brand and what they are achieving. You will learn a lot from them but have your own journey!

Thinking about all this will help you to map your goals for getting there. Your vision can be as grand as you want because then you can scale down when you get to planning. Your vision should make you feel somewhat uncomfortable. To have a grand vision you need to think about your operations and processes. Without these you can't scale. Do revisit your vision as it will evolve and change according to market conditions, what's happening in the business and feedback you get from clients. A vision gives you something to aim for, otherwise you are steering aimlessly.

Values

These are important because you will be recruiting people into the organisation whom you want to strive to meet the values of the organisation. This is called **values-based recruitment**. You can teach knowledge and skills, however, values are intrinsic to us: our drivers, along with our attitudes and behaviours. Think about the values of your organisation. What behaviours do you want from your staff? What are your expectations?

Davies has a great way to make you think about your values. He asks what action of an employee would make you fire them. Look at what behaviours annoy you as this will help to 'flip' what you do value.

One of mine is good time-keeping. I do not like tardiness. I always aim to get to a meeting early, however, if I am going to be late, I inform the person. Values, once known, need to be communicated to staff so that they are aware of what is expected of them. Values also need to be embedded into the organisation – it is no use if the only people who know the values are the business owner and registered manager. All staff need to know and the values should be part of their induction. You need to use your values as part of your recruitment process.

In a small business, it's really important to employ staff who have the same values. You will know very quickly if they don't and if you have employed them you will find either they will leave or you will need to let them go as their values will not be congruent. By recruiting staff who meet your values and the culture of your organisation, it will be enhanced too. Also make sure that other stakeholders, service users and relatives are aware of your values.

I will not work with clients who do not have similar values or who make me uncomfortable because of the values they hold or don't have in some cases. To me my values and integrity are important and if it means not working with the client then I will not! I sleep well knowing I haven't compromised my values.

Your values underpin what your strategy is, so revisit them at least once a year to identify any changes that need to be made. In a crowded marketplace, it's important to stand out from the crowd, so you need to think about what makes you different. In your organisation you make the difference – you are unique. We all need to think about that in terms of how we deliver our services. Think about your unique selling proposition. It could be the technology you use to help support those who use your services, it could be innovative exercise routines. The knowledge and experience of your staff is important.

Strategy

Think about the strategy you will have for your business. Without a strategy, it's like going on a road trip without knowing your destination. If you don't know where you're going how will you know the route and when you have reached your destination? I personally believe it's difficult to plan three or even five years ahead. (Please note, however, that the CQC does require a three-year business plan for those entering the social care sector.) However, planning a year in advance is feasible. If you plan a year ahead on a rolling basis it is more productive as it keeps the business agile and helps you to be responsive and evolve your business to the needs of the service and staff. When I refer to strategy, I talk about a year as long-term, six months as medium-term and three months as short-term. It is actually good to work in three-month cycles as it keeps you focused on your goals. When you are looking at your strategy the core pillars for most small businesses are as follows.

Sales, marketing, operations, finance, human resources

To know where you are with these pillars I recommend starting with a SWOT analysis of each. SWOT stands for Strengths, Weaknesses, Opportunities and Threats. I recommend the layout shown below.

Table 2.2 SWOT Analysis Table

	STRENGTHS *(internal)*	*WEAKNESSES* *(internal)*
OPPORTUNITIES *(external)*	Wealth strategy	Development strategy
THREATS *(external)*	Toughen-up strategy	Critical strategy

Strengths and weakness are internal to the company. Opportunities and threats are external.

- Weaknesses meet threats = critical strategy

- Strengths meet opportunities = wealth strategy

- Weaknesses meet opportunities = development strategy

- Strengths meet threats = toughen-up strategy

Looking at the SWOT analysis in this way will make you think of solutions in a more focused manner because you know which strategy it impacts: critical, wealth development or toughening up, for example. It gives more clarity knowing which boxes items are falling into. Do a SWOT analysis for each of your pillars.

I recommend you take time to do this planning because it will pay dividends in the long term and it will enable you to have clarity on your business.

THREE

Fit and Proper Person

In this chapter I discuss the issue of whether a new provider is fit for purpose to take on the role of nominated individual or registered manager, in relation to the guidelines and requirements laid down by the CQC. Although it is not prosecutable, the CQC can take regulatory action. For this reason it is important to look at this criteria in depth.

When I review a new prospective provider I look at their experience of the sector as well as their qualifications. This is to ensure that the director has the right experience and skills to take on the responsibility of the nominated individual and/or registered manager. I know the application will be rejected if these criteria are not met. I ask questions as to the background they have in the regulated activity – whether it is the health sector or social care sector.

One prospective client came to me and after I had asked a few questions I was candid and said they did not meet Regulation 5 (Fit and Proper Person). All they had was the finances. I suggested they needed to do some personal development work and then come back. Their response did surprise me: the client told me the CQC had told them the exact same thing, but they had not believed them and thought they were just saying that.

I find it astounding when a client has not researched what is needed to be compliant. All they are thinking about is the application. However, the reality is that the application should come *after* due diligence has been done and a structure put in place. Viability should have been looked at and financial forecasts undertaken.

I started my business to ensure that the end-user receives person-centred care. This is achieved by supporting the provider to manage their processes well and ensure they provide adequate training for their staff. I would rather turn a client away and get them to obtain the skills needed than take on an application I know will fail. The reason you need to be a 'fit person' is that a registered manager has joint legal liability with the registered provider for the quality and safety of the services provided. Therefore, this is not to be taken lightly.

Applicants need to have the right knowledge and skills to perform the role of nominated individual and/or registered manager. They also need the right qualifications. For example, in the case of the Adult Social Care sector the inspector will look for the right level of experience or the Level 5 Diploma in Management for Health and Social Care is recommended by Skills for Care (www.skillsforcare.org.uk) for the social care sector, or equivalent experience.

The registered manager has a variety of responsibilities under Regulations 21, 22 and 23 of the Health and Social Care Act 2008 (Regulated Activities) Regulations 2014 in relation to staff. Responsibilities include ensuring that staff have the relevant qualifications, skills, experience and training to carry out the role. Staff in health and adult social care settings should be aware that managers have these responsibilities. They also include appropriate induction and relevant training, including refresher training, support (that might include the use of mentoring/coaching arrangements), supervision and opportunities for staff to reflect on practice in an honest and open manner.

In the health sector you need to be either a medical professional or have the right kind of knowledge and expertise to undertake the role of registered manager. No mandatory qualifications are required for clinics.

In the care sector it is acceptable to be taking Level 5 while you are applying as you have other skills and expertise.

Good managerial skills are easily transferable, especially in the care sector. Experience is also important. The registered manager job is a very challenging role. You are wearing a lot of hats. You need to be a confident and assertive person who can delegate; the job entails spinning many plates. It is also a role that can no longer be done by one person adequately without the help of other staff who can step in while the registered manager is off.

I have a great example of this from a care home group I worked with, and it can apply equally to any sector. The registered manager went on holiday. On her return, the weekly fire test had not been done. A few other areas had not been managed either. It transpired that the registered manager had not managed expectations effectively. She had not advised her senior staff of the full extent of her role. Neither had she given them a checklist of what to do in her absence. She somehow thought they would know what to do. Needless to say, I was able to help them to develop a checklist for when she was away so that tasks were not left untouched. Training and delegation of the seniors also took place.

The next time the registered manager went on holiday she was happy to report that all the necessary tasks had been undertaken. You need to be able to think outside the box. The CQC writes: 'Regulation 5. The intention of this regulation is to ensure that people who have director level responsibility for the quality and safety of care, and for meeting the fundamental standards are fit and proper to carry out this important role.'

The nominated individual, who is usually the owner or delegated person, needs to ensure that they meet the criteria, then in turn that the person they bring in as registered manager is also fit. The organisation will only be able to do this if it has processes in place to check suitability. You need to ensure that all your staff are fit to do their job as well. The CQC will look for adequate systems to be in place.

FOUR

Use the Appropriate Handbook

The CQC now has two handbooks which you need to refer to. One is for health and the other for social care. I have placed links to them below.

If you're a business which sits in the health-care sector http://bit.ly/healthKLOEhandbook. Adult Social Care providers use: http://bit.ly /adultsocialcarehandbook

The handbooks should be used to complete the SOAP because you should be aligning what is required for compliance with the operational activity in the business.

The handbooks outline in detail what is required of the organisation to meet the standards. Use them to formulate your **statement of purpose** which is required by the CQC as part of the application process. It is important to note here that you can buy off-the-shelf policies which meet the standards. However, there is a caveat: these policies, by their very nature, are generic and need to be amended. I have had applicants buy policies and not look at them – it was left to me to read them and attach them to the application. That is very naive and will quickly show the inspectors that you don't know how you are using the policies within the business. Off-the-shelf policies help you to move faster with starting your business, however, you do need to do the groundwork. The handbooks have the KLOE and it is these that the CQC will ask about at inspection and first interview.

The first task is to ensure you are looking at the right handbook. I suggest you sit down with a notebook and write down how you are to meet each criterion. This planning will pay dividends in the long run as it forms the basis for how you will amend the generic policies, plus it will give you the information you need to complete the statement of purpose as well as adhering to the principles of SCREW. Anyone working in the regulated sector must know this. The handbooks are large documents, so I do not recommend downloading them. Do have a look at them section by section – I think it would be useful to put them into a spreadsheet which can then be used for undertaking audits.

While working with the handbooks make sure you are putting in processes to meet the regulations. The KLOE are produced by the CQC and can change, but the regulations are part of the Health and Social Care Act and will not change unless the Act is changed or amended which is usually a very long process. I have listed the regulations below so you can see at a glance which regulations you need to meet:

- Regulation 9: Person-centred care

- Regulation 10: Dignity and respect

- Regulation 11: Need for consent

- Regulation 12: Safe care and treatment

- Regulation 13: Safeguarding service users from abuse and improper treatment

- Regulation 14: Meeting nutritional and hydration needs

- Regulation 15: Premises and equipment

- Regulation 16: Receiving and acting on complaints

- Regulation 17: Good governance

- Regulation 18: Staffing

- Regulation 19: Fit and proper persons employed

- Regulation 20: Duty of candour

FIVE

Modules Within the Application

The online application form consists of the following modules: Who, What, Where, When, How, Documents, Review, and Declaration.

In order to complete the modules efficiently, you will need to do the groundwork first. I find that by doing this you can then input the information for the new provider application form in one sitting.

WHO: Here you are providing information about the nominated individual and registered manager. Part of the process is to invite them also to tell the CQC why they should be the registered manager. Please note even if it is the same person undertaking these two roles the process is to invite them.

WHAT: This informs the CQC which regulated activity you are undertaking and the services you provide.

WHERE: This provides information about the location.

WHEN: When do you wish to start the regulated activity? You must account for the time it takes for the application process when choosing a date.

HOW: You must show you understand the five SCREW domains and how you as an organisation are going to meet each criterion.

DOCUMENTS: In this module there are documents which they ask for, namely the Quality Management System, Safeguarding, Statement of Purpose, Governance Framework, and Registered Manager supporting information.

REVIEW: This stage is to review the application and make any final adjustments.

DECLARATION: This is where you sign the application.

The submission of the new provider application triggers an email from the CQC to the registered manager. (If you are a provider who is an organisation you need to have both a nominated individual and a registered manager.

The registered manager is responsible for the operational running of the regulated activity.) On receiving the email, the registered manager can complete the application within two hours if they have completed the preparation. I have timed myself many times, so I know how much time to set aside.

Preparation is key, otherwise you must keep logging off to go and find the information. The best approach is to find all the information first, then complete the application in one sitting. This way, there is less likelihood of forgetting things and of errors creeping in.

Give yourself plenty of time for preparation. I would say at least two weeks if you're doing it full time or longer if you're fitting it in between other things.

The CQC application itself can take at least twelve weeks from submission to validation. Once you submit your full application, which is both the new provider and the registered manager application, it goes to the main registration office which looks at the application for completeness and can reject it. This can be for a number of reasons, such as incomplete information, lack of information or even if information given does not match the regulated activity for which the application has been made.

If it gets through this stage, it is sent to the regional team who will then send you an email asking for further information. The level and depth of information asked for varies from inspector to inspector – there is no consistency. I find it useful to have a conversation with the inspector – most of them are approachable and building a good rapport with inspectors is essential. They are there to help you and are a good resource. But, as in many other areas, personality plays a large part. The CQC is supposed to train inspectors to be consistent, but I know this is not always the case as I have dealt with inspectors from different regions.

With the application process you do need to be clear on WHAT type of entity you are. Providers do get confused about which they should choose – an individual, partnership or organisation. If you are an organisation you need to know what type. The CQC is also very clear on how you write the 'limited' section of your company name. It must be exactly as it is at Companies House. I advise you to check with Companies House to be certain. The CQC will reject the application for just writing 'Limited' instead of 'Ltd'. I know this seems petty, however, this instruction is very clear on the application. I also know people are not always very good at following this instruction!

Before the application process begins, ensure that the registered manager has applied for the countersigned DBS: Disclosure & Barring Service. For most people this takes about two weeks. The longest I am aware of was eight weeks, so it is best to get it done first. The CQC asks that the DBS has been completed within a year of the application. However, once the DBS is done there is no set time for when a DBS is renewed. Many companies ask for one every three years, check annually that there is no change and ask the employee to sign a declaration.

The WHERE module concerns the location. You need to be clear about this. I have had some simple locations and some complex ones to deal with. For clinics, it is easy if they have one location and it is the same as the registered office. A care home agency may begin by being located at a house until the business has been developed further. This is usually fine, however, there are some caveats. The office area or room has to be separate from the personal side of the house. The room must have a lock or at least have a lockable cabinet to store confidential documents, both for clients and staff. The provider also needs to be clear about how staff will access and how you manage client meetings. They can normally be at their home address as it is more convenient. Decide if you are going to be both nominated individual and registered manager or if you are going to employ someone to do the registered manager role.

The CQC will also want to know that you are financially viable. In the past, businesses have started with not enough cashflow and gone under. The financial viability statement must be completed by an accountant. You will also verify this by sending a copy of the business bank statement when the inspector asks for it.

If you are in a rented office, you need to show that the landlord(s) is in agreement for the regulated activity to be taking place within the premises. This is usually set out in your contract with them, although you do not need to attach it to the application as the inspector will want to be assured that there is a contract when they interview you. It is a question within the application which you need to answer.

If you have had building work done, you must make the premises fit for purpose and you need to state that the landlord has given permission.

A fifth consideration is WHY are you applying for the regulated activity. What is your reason and purpose for doing this? You also need to have an idea of when you want to start the regulated activity. I recommend giving yourself at least three months. By the time the application goes to the CQC, it can take a further ten to twelve weeks. Be realistic: as much as you are eager to start your business, it's more important to make sure you have everything in place.

SIX

Safe, Caring, Responsive, Effective, Well-Led: SCREW

This is the HOW part of the application. If you're using generic off-the-shelf policies, you need to look at what they say and align the policies with how to meet the KLOE. Why? Because what you say you are going to do here aligns with what you actually do. This is operationally reflected in your **statement of purpose**. This document is a 'live' document and you should be looking at it quarterly to make sure you are doing what it says you should.

Safe

The CQC is looking for the systems and processes you have in place to keep people safe. This applies to the start of the recruitment process. You need to consider how you monitor this. How are you managing risk? How will you deal with emergencies? Do your staff have all the information to carry out their role safely? What is your process for record-keeping, both in terms of good record-keeping but also in terms of the management of records for staff as well as patients/service users? How will you manage incident recording? It is important to reflect on what lessons have been learned and how you will disseminate the information.

Caring

How are you as a service going to ensure that people are treated with dignity, kindness and respect? Are you looking at their best interests? Are those you support able to express their views? Are they actively involved in decisions about themselves and the daily running of the service?

Responsive

This involves looking at whether the person-alised care/treatment you provide is right for the people you support. Are reasonable adjustments made for those who find access difficult? The CQC will also want to know that appointments in healthcare are easy to arrange. They will want to know how you deal with compliments and complaints. Complaints need to be embraced and used as a tool for continuous improvement and lessons learned.

Effective

Are you effective as an organisation? Do you know what other regulations you need to meet? You need to be clear on the requirements of the Equality Act and the Mental Capacity Act. How do you monitor care and treatment? Do you benchmark yourself with others?

How are you going to ensure staff, when employed, are going to work in a cohesive way? What is the culture of the organisation? How will you make sure consent is obtained in a positive and responsible manner and understood by your staff?

Well-led

This is the criterion most organisations fail on. Providers appear to lack the knowledge to recognise that managers are not born managers, they need to be trained and be given the right tools to do their role. The organisation also needs to be aware of different models of leadership. **Collective leadership** is an empowering model. This means everyone takes responsibility for the success of the organisation. Leaders and managers create a supportive environment which then leads to staff coming up with solutions to challenges. The King's Fund publication *Developing Collective Leadership for Healthcare* is a good resource for this. The registered manager role has legislation attached to it which means they have a legal duty and responsibility to meet certain regulations. The ultimate penalty is going to prison. Many new providers and registered managers fail to grasp this. The registered manager role is complex and challenging and requires knowledge and experience appropriate to the regulated activity.

For the health sector, health professionals need to have the appropriate qualifications and belong to the relevant professional body, such as the General Dental Council (GDC), the Nursing and Midwifery Council (NMC) or the General Medical Council (GMC).

Qualifications are all well and good but if you cannot apply them in the workplace the qualification is meaningless. The competency of the registered manager has to be checked as much as that of other staff. Remember that all employees need to be fit people to do their job.

Are your staff clear on your vision and strategy? Have they been told what to do? Have you managed their expectations? Is the organisational vision embedded within the organisation or do only senior staff understand it? It should be part of the induction process so that it is embedded within the organisation and its values are apparent daily.

What opportunities are you giving your staff to develop themselves? Not all of this needs to cost a lot of money. Joining forums such as those in relation to infection control in your local area is a good way to keep up to date with good practice. If you have a 'champions' system, each champion can disseminate information and lessons learned to the rest of your team. This is empowering for them and teaches them skills such as presentation and preparation for speaking.

You need to have clear quality assurance systems which demonstrate that you know what you are doing. You need to use the outcomes of audits to improve processes. Continuous improvement should be embedded. There are always ways to improve. It does not have to be big changes either. I helped a senior executive to be more effective by managing expectations and setting what I call 'office hours'. She has reported that there have been improvements in her effectiveness due to this small change. She has been able to get more tasks completed. Now she only replies to emails at certain times of the day. Her productivity has improved. This has also empowered her staff as they have learned to take decisions rather than running to the senior executive. A good leader knows how to delegate and to empower their staff to be leaders themselves. Staff should be encouraged to resolve problems together and be given the space to make mistakes and learn from them.

SEVEN

Application Documents

There are documents you must attach with your application. Completing these is a priority.

I have already discussed the statement of purpose and information on this is available on the CQC website. The CQC provides advice on what you need to include. I recommend you complete this statement before you begin your application. For the social care sector, the CQC also requires a three-year business plan. This is not attached to the application but, on accepting the application, the CQC will ask for the business plan and forecast. The cashflow forecast can be a table within the plan – it does not have to be a separate document.

The quirk of the CQC application platform is that you can't add multiple documents. Therefore, I merge the documents which form part of the Quality Management System into one Word document and then convert this to a PDF (portable document format file). The CQC requires the policies related to your quality management system; these include details of health and safety arrangements, incident report-ing, complaints procedures, audits, infection control measures, record-keeping, recruitment, appraisal and your induction policy. Other standalone policies are safeguarding, and the governance policy or framework, depending on the category of business you are operating in. There are two other policy issues concerning premises, however, these are optional and therefore I never use them. All the documents are restricted in their file size so using PDF format is better and also means that document formatting won't be affected.

You must remember that when you change your statement of purpose you need to notify the CQC every time such changes are made. A section of the application refers to the 'registered manager supporting document'. This document is written to support the manager's application. In many cases the nominated individual and the registered manager are one and the same, but you must write this section in the second person and include 'their' knowledge and skills and what makes 'them' a fit person for the role. It is important to include any relevant qualifications here.

On completing the new provider application, check for accuracy and then sign the declaration and submit. There is an opportunity to download the PDF of your application. I recommend you do this as you will need it for interview so that you remember what you wrote.

EIGHT

The Registered Manager Application

When you press the send button for your new provider application, the registered manager will receive an email asking them to submit their application for the management of the regulated activity. Choose your registered manager wisely – they are legally responsible and need to understand the complexity of the registered manager role.

Skills for Care says the following are important:

- Governance and accountability

- Team leadership and management

- Managing resources

- Equality, diversity and inclusion

- Safeguarding and protection

- Ensuring quality

- Training and development

In order to prepare for the registered manager application there are four key pieces of information required: countersigned DBS, employment history, GP details/medical history, and referee(s).

The countersigned DBS needs to be valid within a year of submitting the application. You will need a fifteen-year employment history for the application, however, for recruitment of your staff a full employment history is required as per Schedule 3, accounting for any gaps in employment. The reason for this mismatch is that the CQC has not (at the time of writing) updated the electronic application. There is a format to completing this information. I find that if you have it all in place on your CV it makes the task that much simpler. The format is:

- Start date: dd /mm/yyyy
- End date: dd/mm/yyyy
- Tasks done in the role
- Reason for leaving

For any gaps, you still require the same information. Use the format as above (eg unemployed, taking a year out, travelling, maternity etc). Many applicants fail because they do not account for the 15-year history and any gaps.

Your GP details should include the first name and surname, plus the address and phone number of the surgery. You need to declare any medical conditions which may affect your ability to do the job. The CQC needs to be made aware of significant health conditions, including any mental health issues.

For your referee(s) you need to provide the following information:

- Full name

- Address

- Email

- Phone contact number

Any supporting information must state why this person (ie you or another person) is suitable for the role of registered manager. I usually use the same information as that used in the registered manager's supporting information in the new provider application.

Once you have completed this application fully you will receive an email from the CQC once the head office team have looked at your application. All correspondence from the CQC is via email. Therefore it is vital that you give them the address you look at daily and is active.

NINE

Getting Ready for Initial Review/Interview

Once you have submitted your application you need to prepare for the initial interview. The interview will either take place over the phone or face to face. You will be assigned a regional inspector who will write to you and ask for further information. The questions they ask are to determine that you are a fit person to undertake the role of registered manager.

They will also want to speak with the nominated individual. You need to know about the KLOE, safeguarding and data protection. You also need to know what is in the statement of purpose and your governance document, how will you deal with incidents, emergencies etc. The CQC can ask about anything really, but I have found from what people have said in forums that these are the key areas.

Remember, you have done all the groundwork. Make sure you have a locked cabinet for confidential records; if you are employing staff, purchase a poster from the Health and Safety Executive (HSE) website concerning health and safety law. Make sure that in any clinical areas a handwashing poster/guidance is clearly displayed.

If you are in rented accommodation, make sure you know what the fire safety rules are for the building. I also recommend you have your qualification certificates in a folder.

If you hold your policies electronically, don't print them all. Instead, ensure you have a guest access code or password for the inspector to log in and view these documents. Stay calm and answer any questions truthfully. If you don't know, say you will find out.

TEN

Post Registration

Once you are registered, the journey begins. What you need to do is evidence everything you do. My motto is 'Say what you do, do what you say and show what you do'. Appropriate evidence is a key factor. You need to perform audits on a regular basis. Don't try to do them all in one month as this is not effective. Do an audit each month. Vary the areas you audit – some areas may require auditing more frequently. Use the KLOE as guidance. The CQC will inspect you twelve months after registration to give you time to embed your processes. You should be able to show what the actuals are against your initial forecasts in terms of your financial forecasts. The CQC will want to know that staffing levels are adequate.

Remember you need to market your services where your clients are likely to see them. You need to look at a marketing strategy. I see too many providers jump straight into tactics when they need to be looking at strategy. Networking is a great way to meet ideal clients, but it should be part of your strategy.

Do register for the CQC newsletter as it's a good source of information. Register with the Information Commissioner's Office (ICO) also to fulfil your duty under GDPR. Sign up for the ICO newsletter as well.

Enjoy the journey and don't run before you can walk. Be realistic about what you can achieve. The information in this guide should help you to make an outstanding application and provide you with the right start for your regulated activity organisation.

Further Reading

BGI Strategy on a Page, Deri ap John Llewellyn Davies (Filament Publishing, UK 2013)

Developing Collective Leadership for Healthcare, Michael West, Regina Eckert, Katy Stewart, Bill Pasmore, The King's Fund, May 2014

Acknowledgements

Many thanks to:

Lucy McCarraher, who has been a brilliant book coach;

Lucy Barkas, Janet Swift and Anne Whitehouse, who are part of my ABOO (A Book Of One's Own #1Circle) and held my hand throughout the process;

Geri Connelly, my beta reader and mentee, who understands this sector well;

Ravi Bains of Grosvenor HSC, who has always
been encouraging;

My friend Prabhjit Boparai, for always believ-
ing in me;

My clients, who have inspired me to write this
book;

Ravi Gowda, for writing my Foreword.

The Author

 A British immigrant born in Nairobi in 1963, I came here in January 1968, just as Enoch Powell was debating immigration in the House of Commons.

I never had a career goal and was never encouraged by the school system, perhaps because I came from a council estate and went to a state school. However, I have always felt there was more and once my children started full time school, I got a job at the local hospital. I believe that if you have children you should look after them. My mum did and that's what I wanted to do. I joined the NHS and worked my way up, taking opportunities as they were presented. I am a firm believer that if you don't ask you don't get.

I started my consulting business in 2012. It made sense for me to have a business in the field I knew about and felt comfortable in. My business has developed, and I love mentoring which I fell into. I didn't even realise that was what I was doing until I met Kerri Dorman of the Association of Business Mentors. She told me that I was in fact mentoring. She invited me to an Association of Business Mentors conference which had a great impact on me and I thought, 'This is what I want to do.' I absolutely love what I do. Being able to support people to be more effective and efficient and helping them to see a problem in a different way really inspires me.

To get in touch with me please visit my website:

🌐 www.tchauhanconsultancy.co.uk
✉ taruna@tchauhanconsultancy.co.uk

Printed in Great Britain
by Amazon